Alexander the Grape

fruit and vegetable jokes

compiled by Charles Keller
illustrated by Gregory Filling

Prentice-Hall, Inc./Englewood Cliffs, New Jersey

For Nicole and Leigh

Text copyright © 1982 by Charles Keller
Illustrations copyright © 1982 by Gregory Filling
All rights reserved. No part of this book may be
reproduced in any form, or by any means,
except for the inclusion of brief quotations in a review,
without permission in writing from the publisher.
Printed in the United States of America · J
Prentice-Hall International, Inc., London
Prentice-Hall of Australia, Pty. Ltd., North Sydney
Prentice-Hall of Canada, Ltd., Toronto
Prentice-Hall of India Private Ltd., New Delhi
Prentice-Hall of Japan, Inc., Tokyo
Prentice-Hall of Southeast Asia Pte. Ltd., Singapore
Whitehall Books Limited, Wellington, New Zealand

10 9 8 7 6 5 4 3 2
10 9 8 7 6 5 4   (pbk.)

Library of Congress Cataloging in Publication Data
Keller, Charles. Alexander the Grape
and other fruit and vegetable jokes.
Summary: A collection of humorous riddles
incorporating fruits and vegetables, such as, "What's
a raisin? A worried grape."
1. Riddles, Juvenile. 2. Wit and humor, Juvenile.
3. Fruit—Anecdotes, facetiae, satire, etc.
4. Vegetables—Anecdotes, facetiae, satire, etc.
(1. Riddles) I. Filling, Gregory, ill. II. Title.
PN6371.5.K38 1982   818'.5402   81-19265
ISBN 0-13-021410-8   AACR2
ISBN 0-13-020918-X (pbk.)

What's purple and conquered the world?
Alexander the Grape.

Why aren't bananas ever lonely?
Because they come in bunches.

What's the best way to keep dried prunes?
Don't return them.

How do bananas attract other bananas?
With a-peel.

How do you make gold stew?
Add fourteen carrots.

What's green and very dangerous?
A herd of stampeding pickles.

What's purple and lights up?
The electric grape.

Why are cherries red?
So you can tell them from watermelons.

**What do you get when you cross a potato
with an onion?**
A potato with watery eyes.

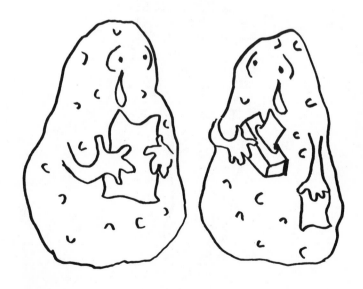

What's very tall and orange?
The Empire State Carrot.

What do you get when you cross a tree with a genius?
Albert Pinestein.

Why did the cornstalk get mad at the farmer?
He kept pulling its ears.

How does a ghost eat an apple?
By goblin it.

What's green and black and blue?
A bruised pickle.

What do two bananas do when they meet
each other?
A banana shake.

What's green and bores holes?
A drill pickle.

Can you eat grapes with fingers?
No, grapes don't have fingers.

What do you get when the Jolly Green
Giant steps on your house?
Mushed rooms.

What do you call cabbages that talk a lot?
Gabbages.

What would you have if you had 50 apples, 40 pears, and 30 oranges?
A fruit stand.

What's yellow and seldom rings?
An unlisted banana.

What's Newton's Law?
One fig to every cookie.

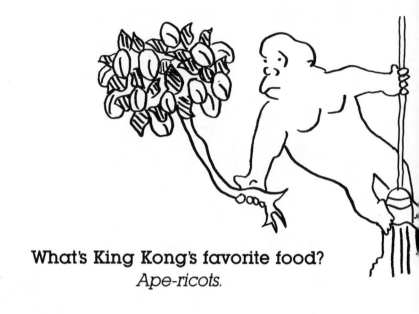

What's King Kong's favorite food?
Ape-ricots.

When is an apple a grouch?
When it's a crab apple.

What's green and writes music?
Johann Sebastian Broccoli.

Why didn't the lemon cross the road?
Because it was yellow.

What's round, purple, and carries a
machine gun?
Al Ca-plum.

What animals failed to come to Noah's
ark in pairs?
Worms. They came in apples.

What's purple and surrounded by water?
Grape Britain.

What's a vampire's favorite fruit?
A neck-tarine.

Why did the tomato go out with the prune?
Because he couldn't find a date.

Who is the pickle's favorite gangster?
John Dill-inger.

When are vegetables like music?
When there are two beets to the measure.

What's purple and 5,000 miles long?
The Grape Wall of China.

What does an orange do on the breakfast table?
It just sits there and looks round.

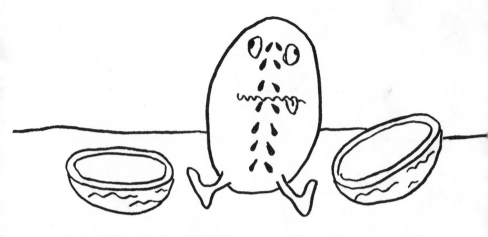

When do you know that a watermelon is crazy?
When it's out of its rind.

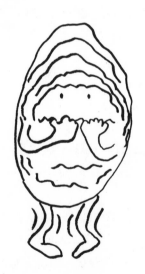

What's a raisin?
A worried grape.

What's green and goes clomp, clomp?
A pickle trying out his new combat boots.

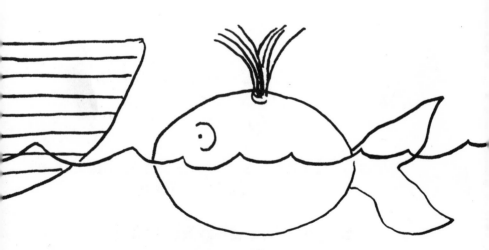

What's purple and swims?
Moby Grape.

What's worse than a worm in an apple?
Half a worm.

What's the difference between an elephant and a grape?
The grape is purple.

What did one baby corn say to the other?
"The stalk brought me."

What's yellow, then purple, then yellow, then purple?
A banana that works part time as a grape.

What's red and lives under the sea?
An apple in a submarine.

What did the baby chick say when it saw the orange in its mother's nest?
"Look at the orange mama-laid."

What's the difference between a yam and a television announcer?
One is a sweet potato and the other is a common-tater.

What's another name for a vegetarian?
A good salad citizen.

If a carrot and a cabbage had a race,
who would win?
The cabbage, because it's ahead.

What do you get when you cross a potato
with a sponge?
*A potato that tastes awful but sure soaks up a
lot of gravy.*

What has 1,000 seeds and moves by itself?
A remote-controlled fig.

What's yellow and carries a basket of
eggs?
The Easter Banana.

What did one carrot say to the other carrot?
Nothing, carrots can't talk.

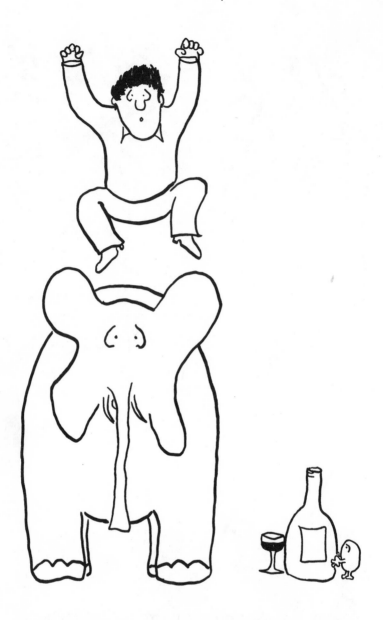

How can you tell the difference between
an elephant and a grape?
*Jump around on it awhile. If you don't get
any wine, it's an elephant.*

What do you call an apple that plays the trumpet?
A tooty fruity.

What room can be eaten?
A mushroom.

What kind of shoes are made of banana skins?
Slippers.

What's yellow and goes, "Ho, ho, ho"?
Santa Banana.

What has a yellow dress, yellow hair, yellow shoes, and yellow skin?
Little Orphan Banannie.

What's yellow, shoots webs, and jumps from building to building?
Spider Yam.

What do you get when you stuff a turkey
with apples?
An apple gobbler.

What's the most dangerous vegetable to
have on a boat?
A leek.

What's yellow and points north?
A magnetic banana.

What's yellow, rides a white horse, and
shoots silver bullets?
The Lone Lemon.

Why do grapes come in bunches?
So they can get their sneakers wholesale.

What's yellow and furry?
A peach with a mink stole.

Why shouldn't you tell secrets on a farm?
Because the corn has ears, the potatoes have eyes, and the beans talk.

Why don't you ever see an elephant in a strawberry patch?
Because she paints her toenails red.

What would you have if plants had CB radios?

Interplantery communication.

What fruit did Noah take on the ark?
Pairs.

What vegetable do you get when you
drop a tomato?
Squash.

What do you call a pickle that can add,
subtract, multiply, and divide?
A cuculator.

Why did the cabbage leaf?
Because it saw the banana split.

What fruit is on a dime?
A date.

What kind of beans do werewolves eat?
Human beans.

What's red and eats oranges?
A red orange-eater.

Why do watermelons contain so much water?
They are planted in the spring.

Why did the orange stop in the middle of
the road?
It ran out of juice.

What's red and goes through walls?
Casper the friendly strawberry.

What side of an apple is the left side?
The side you haven't eaten.

What does an apple have that no other
fruit has?
Apple seeds.

What do you call a twisted path through an Indian cornfield?
A maize.

Why is a tomato the exact opposite of a traffic light?
You must wait for the tomato to turn from green to red and the traffic light to turn from red to green.

What kind of vegetable can put air in a football?
A pumpkin.

What's the first words at a pickle wedding ceremony?

Dilly beloved.

How is a banana peel on a sidewalk like music?
Because if you don't C sharp, you'll B flat.

What does a peanut become when it sneezes?
A cashew.

What do you get when you cross a watermelon with a greyhound?
A watermelon that seats 45 people.

818   8/92   Keller, Charles.
KEL   8/92   Alexander the Grape

$9.15   240 7517

DATE DUE		PERMA-BOUND	